The Aztecs

THE ANCIENT WORLD

The Aztecs

Pamela Odijk

Silver Burdett Press

Acknowledgments

The author and publishers are grateful to the following for permission to reproduce copyright photographs and prints:

ANT/G. D. Anderson p. 34; ANT/Davidson Bishop p. 12; ANT/NHPA p. 11; Bettman Archive p. 40; Bibliocteca Universitaria Di Bologna, Italy p. 32; National Museums & Galleries of Merseyside, Liverpool p. 26; South American Pictures p. 10; Werner Forman Archive pp. 13, 15, 16, 20, 21 right, 22, 23, 25, 27, 33, 36 and the cover photograph.

While every care has been taken to trace and acknowledge copyright, the publishers tender their apologies for any accidental infringement where copyright has proven untraceable. They would be pleased to come to a suitable arrangement with the rightful owner in each case.

First published 1989 by
THE MACMILLAN COMPANY OF AUSTRALIA PTY LTD
107 Moray Street, South Melbourne 3205
6 Clarke Street, Crows Nest 2065

Adapted and first published in the United States in 1990 by Silver Burdett Press, Englewood Cliffs, N.J.

Library of Congress Cataloging-in-Publication Data

Odijk, Pamela, 1942–
    The Aztecs.
    (The Ancient world)
    Summary: Surveys the culture, government, religion, and achievements of the Aztecs and the collapse of their empire with the arrival of the Spanish under Cortez.
    1. Aztecs—Juvenile literature. [1. Aztecs] I. Title. II. Series: Odijk, Pamela, 1942–   Ancient world.
F1219.73.O55 1990   972'.018   89-24197
    ISBN 0-382-09887-0

The Aztecs

Contents

The Aztecs: Timeline

Before the end of the last Ice Age, Siberia and Alaska were joined by a landbridge. The American Indians migrated from Asia in search of animals. Gradually these first migrants moved south into Mexico and South America.

50,000 B.C.	20,000

Many of the farming communities had become towns built around the central lake. The people built huge flat-topped pyramids with temples on top. These towns became religious centers.

1500 B.C.	1400	1300	1200	1100	1000	900 B.C.	A.D. 600

Olmec civilization in Mexico. Great sculptures of heads in Southern Mexico were carved by the Olmecs. The Olmec civilization developed a calendar and a counting system. The Olmecs also built huge pyramids in Central Mexico.

A.D.	1440	1460	1480

Montezuma I was King of the Aztecs. During his reign great aqueducts were built to bring fresh water from the mainland for the growing island city. Parts of the island were reclaimed. The Aztec empire expanded into the south and the Gulf coast.

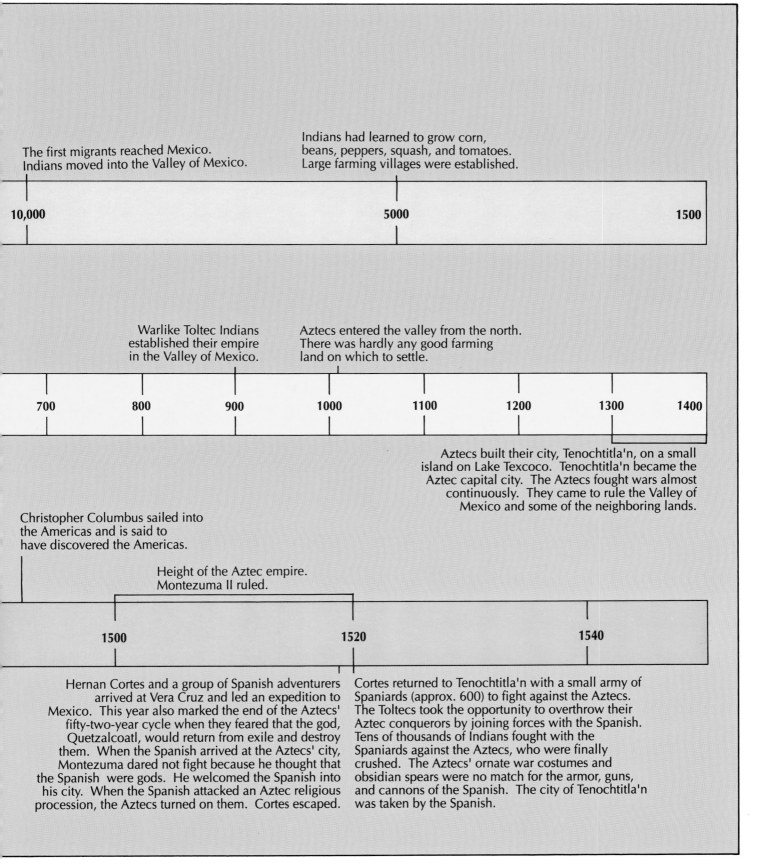

The first migrants reached Mexico.
Indians moved into the Valley of Mexico.

Indians had learned to grow corn,
beans, peppers, squash, and tomatoes.
Large farming villages were established.

10,000	5000	1500

Warlike Toltec Indians
established their empire
in the Valley of Mexico.

Aztecs entered the valley from the north.
There was hardly any good farming
land on which to settle.

700	800	900	1000	1100	1200	1300	1400

Aztecs built their city, Tenochtitla'n, on a small
island on Lake Texcoco. Tenochtitla'n became the
Aztec capital city. The Aztecs fought wars almost
continuously. They came to rule the Valley of
Mexico and some of the neighboring lands.

Christopher Columbus sailed into
the Americas and is said to
have discovered the Americas.

Height of the Aztec empire.
Montezuma II ruled.

1500	1520	1540

Hernan Cortes and a group of Spanish adventurers arrived at Vera Cruz and led an expedition to Mexico. This year also marked the end of the Aztecs' fifty-two-year cycle when they feared that the god, Quetzalcoatl, would return from exile and destroy them. When the Spanish arrived at the Aztecs' city, Montezuma dared not fight because he thought that the Spanish were gods. He welcomed the Spanish into his city. When the Spanish attacked an Aztec religious procession, the Aztecs turned on them. Cortes escaped.

Cortes returned to Tenochtitla'n with a small army of Spaniards (approx. 600) to fight against the Aztecs. The Toltecs took the opportunity to overthrow their Aztec conquerors by joining forces with the Spanish. Tens of thousands of Indians fought with the Spaniards against the Aztecs, who were finally crushed. The Aztecs' ornate war costumes and obsidian spears were no match for the armor, guns, and cannons of the Spanish. The city of Tenochtitla'n was taken by the Spanish.

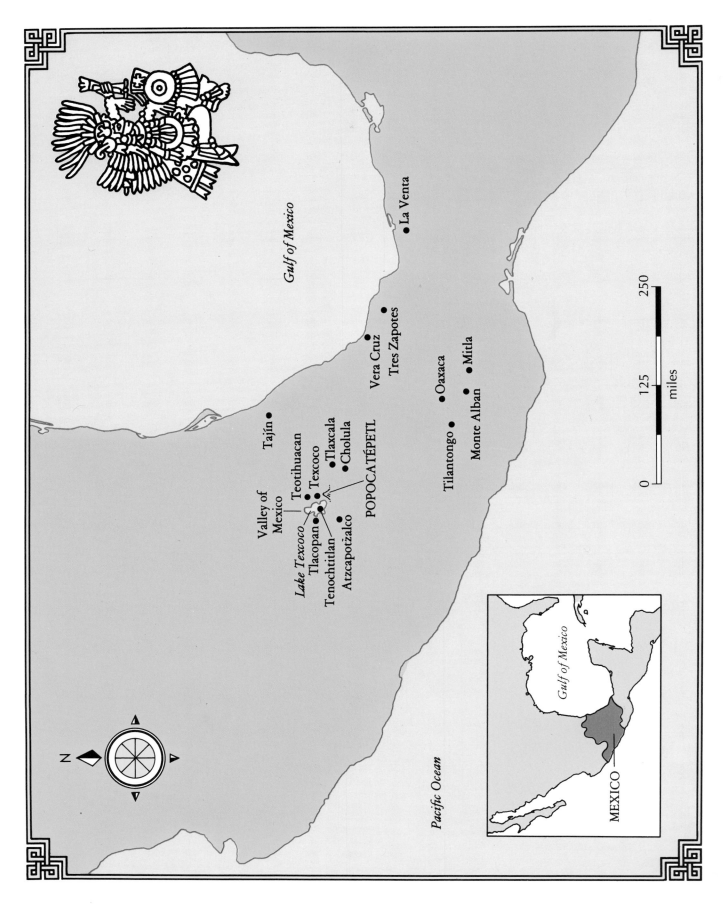

Gulf of Mexico

La Venta

Tajín

Vera Cruz
Tres Zapotes

Teotihuacan
Texcoco
Tlaxcala
Cholula

Valley of
Mexico

POPOCATÉPETL

Lake Texcoco
Tlacopan
Tenochtitlan
Atzcapotzalco

Tilantongo

Oaxaca
Mitla

Monte Alban

Pacific Ocean

MEXICO

Gulf of Mexico

0   125   250

miles

N

8

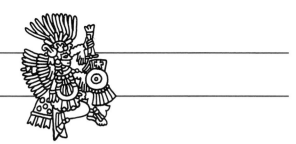

The Aztecs: Introduction

The Aztecs believed that they were the chosen people of their patron god, Huitzilopochtli (Blue Hummingbird). They were nomadic people whose wanderings from about A.D. 1168 finally led them to settle in the Basin of Mexico, where they built their city on the lake's islands. Though the Aztecs lived for some time as farmers under the rule of others, they soon began a series of conquests in the name of the sun god, Tonatiuh. In the fifteenth and sixteenth centuries A.D., the Aztecs ruled a large empire in what is now called southern Mexico. The Aztecs were also called the Tenocha (after an ancestor, Tenoch) and the Mexica. They ruled their empire from the capital, Tenochtitlán, a huge city covering 5 square miles (13 square kilometers). The Aztec capital was originally two separate cities, Tlatelolco and Tenochtitlán, but these were merged into one.

The Aztecs made the lands productive by using good farming techniques and irrigation systems. They reclaimed much land. However, their lands could not produce all the resources they needed, so the Aztecs moved out to conquer other lands.

The Aztecs spoke the Nahuatl language, which was common to all the valley people. They thought of themselves as "the people of the sun" and believed that the sun would disappear from the heavens if it was not given human hearts. Because of this belief sacrifices were a regular and central part of their religious ceremonies. The Aztecs worshiped many gods, some of which were adopted from the religions of conquered people.

When the Spanish arrived, looking for riches, the Aztec empire extended over most of central Mexico. The Spanish, under Hernan Cortes, eventually conquered the Aztec lands, capturing the capital city in A.D. 1521. The Spanish killed many Aztecs during the years of conquest: in battle and by introducing diseases to which the Aztecs had no resistance. Aztec documents, records, and works of art were also destroyed by the Spanish. The Spanish introduced their own religion and customs and prevailed upon the Aztecs to accept them. Gradually the old Aztec religion, customs, and culture were changed and almost disappeared.

Our information about the Aztecs comes from the writings of the Spanish whose documentation is based on the Aztec books and from their observations. The Aztecs had many records and books about their civilization, but the Spanish destroyed most of these. A few have survived, which tell us something of how the Aztecs viewed their own culture.

Miniature mask that is thought to represent Huitzilopochtli's lieutenant, Ixtilton.

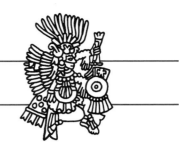

The Importance of Landforms and Climate

The Aztec lands were in the Mexico Valley, a huge basin 7,218 feet (2,200 meters) above sea level and surrounded by high mountains, the peaks of which reach a height of 18,045 feet (5,500 meters) and include the volcano of Popocatépetl. Because most of the land is on a slope much erosion occurs. Also, there are many lakes and much of the land adjacent to the lakes is waterlogged.

Rainfall varies from 20 to 35 inches (500 to 900 mm) in the valley to 50 inches (1,300 mm) on the hillsides, with most rain falling between May and October. In the higher areas, frosts are severe and last for many months. Although the area receives a high rainfall, it is unreliable, and delayed rains and frosts ruin many crops.

The Aztecs developed a number of ways to farm their land. They terraced the sloping lands so water would not wash away the soil and crops. They fertilized the soil with animal manure and used **dry farming** techniques. They also reclaimed a great deal of swamp land by building **chinampas** ("floating gardens"). They controlled the flooding by digging ditches and building dikes, canals, and **sluicegates.** Even part of the saltwater lake, Lake Texcoco, was converted to a freshwater bay by extracting the salt.

Obsidian (which was used for tools and weapons), basalt soil, and rock (for millstones and sculptures) were mined. Although iron ore was also available, its use and value were not known to the Aztecs.

The Aztecs terraced their sloping lands.

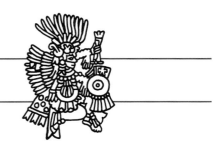

Natural Plants, Animals, and Birds

Pine forests grew on the high slopes. Timber supplies were obtained from these slopes. The **maguey cactus** grew wild and was cultivated, along with cotton. Animals such as deer, **coyotes,** hares, rabbits, and **ocelots** lived in the forest areas, along with many birds, including the **quetzal** and hummingbird. Most of the native animals and birds were hunted. The area's waterfowl and fish were trapped, netted, and speared, and used for food and clothing.

The quetzal bird, prized for its tail feather.

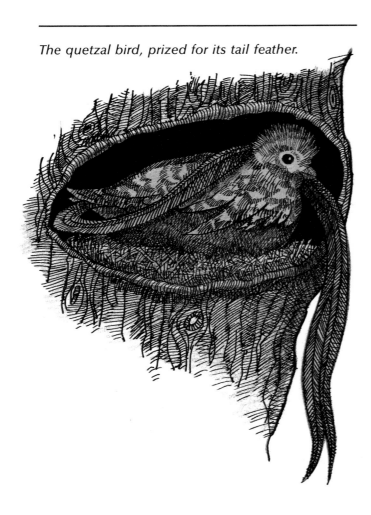

The coyote inhabited the forested areas of the Aztec lands.

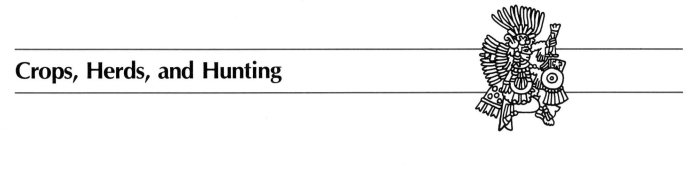

Crops, Herds, and Hunting

Families were organized into groups called a **calpulli** (community), which was given land to be distributed among its members. The calpulli could be a small isolated community surrounded by land, or a group of houses distributed over a region.

Farmers had no draft animals and land was cultivated with a digging stick called a **coa,** which looked like a spade and hoe combined. Farming methods varied from one region to another.

Opposite: cacti grew wild in the Aztec lands.

Below: Xochimilco to the south of Mexico City. This is all that remains of the chinampas, the Aztecs' floating gardens.

Along the Gulf Coast a method of farming known as shifting agriculture was practiced. A patch of forest would be cleared and sown with crops. When the soil lost its fertility after a few years, a new patch of forest would be cleared and cultivated.

Intensive agriculture of a more permanent nature was practiced in the highlands, but crops often failed because the rainfall was insufficient. In times of drought the people often sold themselves into slavery. Plagues of locusts and rats also destroyed the crops.

Chinampa farming was a specialized form of farming and is still in practice today. Each chinampa was built up as a small island using vegetation, dirt, and mud, and became a small, artificial, stationary island, which was intensively farmed. Sides of the chinampas were held in place by posts, which supported a frame. Trees with roots were planted to improve the soil's concentration. Sometimes chinampas were built on rafts so they could be towed from place to place.

The main crop was maize and many varieties were grown. Seed was saved from the previous harvest and taken to the temple to be blessed at the feast of the maize goddess before sowing. Special maize cakes were made from the crop and eaten during the festival of Xilonen, goddess of young corn and first fruits. When the crop was ripe, the ears were harvested and tied into bundles ready for use. Vegetables of many kinds were also grown.

Markets

In smaller towns, markets were held in open plazas every fifth day, and, in larger towns and cities, every day. Some markets were very large. The market at Tlatelolco had 60,000 buyers and sellers on the main market day.

Hundreds of canoes and rafts brought goods to the markets.

Hunting

Common people hunted for food. The largest animal hunted was the white-tailed deer. Hunters used a camouflage of skins and branches to approach their prey, which were killed with arrows. Other animals and birds were lured with decoy whistles. Rabbits, hares, and coyotes were caught in nets. Pits camouflaged with sticks, nets, and grass were also used to trap animals. Waterbirds were caught in the rivers with traps and nets. Fish were speared with a **trident.** The skins and furs of animals were used and traded. Ocelots were hunted to make ceremonial clothing for warriors.

Wealthier people often hunted quails and pigeons, using blowpipes which fired small arrows and pellets to kill the birds.

This codex shows the textures of the maize plant, which is healthy on the right, though in poor condition on the left.

How Families Lived

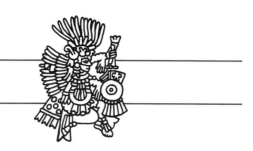

Country Peasant Houses

Rural families lived in groups, and often, up to three families might occupy one house with apartments. Houses were small **adobe** or stone houses arranged around a courtyard. Walls of stone and mud would be built upon a stone foundation. Roofs were thatched. Reed mats covered the floor upon which people sat and slept. Wooden chests and baskets were used for storage.

Town Dwellings of the Wealthy

Wealthy people lived in multi-roomed houses of one or two stories, which stood on high platforms. Walls were made of adobe and covered with plaster. Roofs were flat and covered with wooden planks. Earth was spread over the planks so roof gardens could be grown. Walls that faced the street were blank and rooms opened onto a courtyard. Floors were made of cement. Awnings and curtains provided shade and decoration.

Furniture was simple and mainly consisted of raised wooden platforms and benches with the occasional stool. Carved, gilded screens divided rooms. Other furnishings consisted of baskets and chests for storage, plain basic pottery, and cups and vases of lacquered wood. All houses had images of the gods.

Most people living in the towns were craftsmen, priests, warriors, and administrators.

An eating bowl and two drinking cups. This more sophisticated type of pottery probably was used by noblemen and priests.

Women

Women took part in social and working life, and retained certain rights after marriage. Women served in the temples but were not allowed to perform sacrifices.

Apart from domestic work, women also worked in industry and on the farm. Women were the spinners and weavers in the textile industry. Cotton was obtained from the ripe bolls of the cotton plant. Maguey leaves were processed to produce a linenlike thread that could be woven into cloth. Dyes—indigo, yellow, red, green, and purple—were made from plants, minerals, and shellfish. Looms ranged from very simple belt looms to large streamlined looms on which complicated designs and patterns could be produced. Women were also tailors and seamstresses.

Education

Boys and girls of the middle and upper classes were educated by priests and priestesses. They were taught the routines of the temple. At the **cálmecac,** or higher school, children were taught how to interpret hieroglyphics, astronomy, and natural science, government, and administration. Punishments for misbehavior were severe.

Opposite: seated figure of Xuihtecuhtli, Lord of Fire, who represented the great creator, Ometecuhtli, and was present in the hearth of every home.

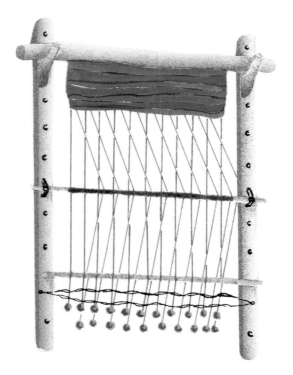

Loom used for weaving cloth. The women were the spinners and weavers in the textile industry.

Gold miners

Gold was brought to the Aztecs from distant provinces. Most gold came from Zacatula, where it was washed from the river bed using **gourds** and wooden boxes. Sometimes gold was melted down in pottery vessels. It was then transported to metalworkers in the city, who sometimes added copper to it.

Calpulli

All families were organized into groups or communities called calpulli. Each calpulli was ruled by the heads of all the households in the calpulli. The calpulli paid taxes in the form of food grown or textiles woven by the women. The calpulli also worked as a labor force. In towns, the calpulli became units of craft specialization. Each calpulli had a school for young men, called a **telpochcalli,** for military and moral instruction.

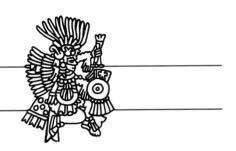

Food and Medicine

Peasant Families

For the common people maize was the main food. Maize was boiled, shucked, and ground into flour using a handstone and a slab called a metate. Maize was used to make **tortillas** (a type of pancake) and porridge. Food was cooked on a **hearth** of stones over which a clay disk called a comal rested.

Turkeys, ducks, game, and a specially bred, hairless dog were the main sources of meat, though meat was a luxury for the Aztecs. Most meals contained a variety of vegetables chosen from tomatoes, squash, beans, green and red peppers, avocado, **papaya,** and **granadilla.**

Tamales were made from crushed maize and red peppers steamed in maize husks. Tamales could also be made with mushrooms, fruit, and fish. The Aztecs also ate frogs, snails, lizards, tadpoles, grubs, and water flies.

The first meal of the day was eaten mid-morning and usually consisted of maize porridge sweetened with honey or spiced with **pimento.** The main meal of the day was eaten at mid-day.

Most people drank water but an alcoholic drink made from the maguey plant was also drunk.

Wealthy Families

The wealthier families ate more elaborate meals, which included foods brought in from other provinces, such as pineapples, sweet potatoes, oysters, crabs, and sea fish. They also drank chocolatl, made from cocoa beans and flavored with vanilla. Wealthy families entertained at banquets, where a variety of dishes were served.

Woman making tortillas.

Medicine

In many ancient societies, including the Aztec society, medicine was a part of religion and magic. Priests were the people concerned with healing and cures. The Aztecs gave the name of **tititl** to a healer. Sickness was believed to have been sent by the gods, who would then have to be appeased by the offering of human sacrifices and the wearing of amulets.

The Aztecs made some advances in medicine. Medicines were made from herbs and plants, and dressings were applied to wounds. Massage was used and dislocated limbs were manipulated back into place. Wounds were sewn up with hair.

Dental health was considered important. People cleaned their teeth with salt and powdered charcoal. Treatments were available for toothaches, and teeth could be extracted.

Hospitals were established in cities to care for the sick and for disabled warriors.

Peyote cactus

Indian turnip

Jimson weed

Juniper

Herbs and some animals were used to cure people with diseases.

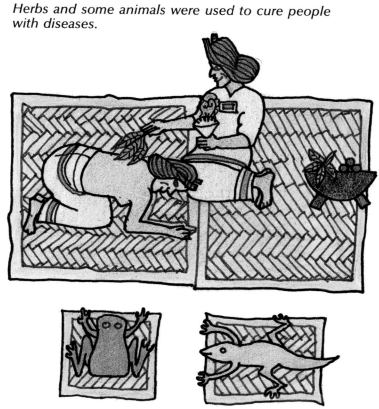

Frog   *Lizard*

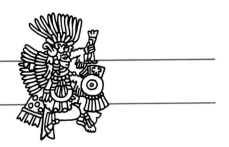

Clothes

Men

Men wore a loin cloth, which was knotted in front and behind. The ends of the loin cloth were often decorated with jewels and feathers. Farmers and workmen wore loin cloths made from maguey fiber, and embroidered cotton was worn by the nobility. Boys wore a loin cloth from four years of age onwards.

A cloak was a symbol of wealth, and rich men wore several at once. The cloak was a rectangular piece of material wound around the body, under the left armpit and knotted over the right shoulder. The cloaks of poor men were plain, while cloaks of the rich were elaborately woven with borders of feathers or fur.

Priests and warriors wore knee-length tunics. The ceremonial dress of an Aztec warrior was very elaborate. It indicated rank and ability in battle. The ceremonial dress of a priest was also elaborate. Priests often assumed the appearance of a god. Priests dressed in black and painted their bodies black too. The body paint contained stimulating substances that enabled the priests to dance for days at religious ceremonies.

Certain designs and insignia were used to show a wearer's status. Turquoise was the color worn by the king.

Most people went barefoot, although sol-

Featherwork shield believed to have belonged to Montezuma's great uncle.

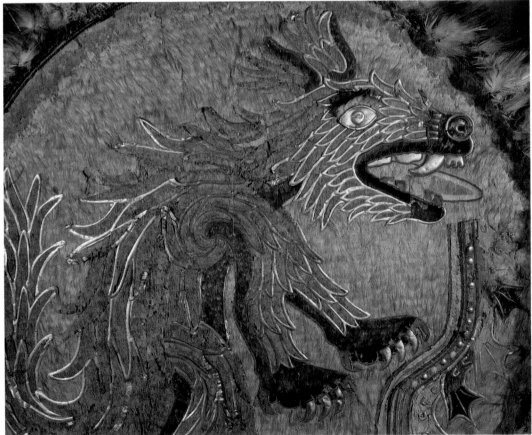

diers and wealthier people wore sandals of leather or plaited grass.

Women

Women wore long skirts fastened at the waist with an embroidered belt. Skirts for everyday use were plain, while those worn at festivals were elaborately embroidered. Over the skirt a simple blouse called a huipil was worn. A huipil was made from a rectangular piece of cloth with holes for the head and arms. This garment was often embroidered at the neck and border hem.

Hair

Men cut their coarse, straight, black hair in a fringe across the forehead. The length of a man's hair was never longer than the nape of the neck. Women grew their hair long and wore it either loose or braided with ribbons. Priests had special, distinctive hairstyles and warriors wore pigtails or special hair tufts to indicate their status.

Above: a back shield worn by a nobleman representing the feathered serpent. The shield is decorated with turquoise, red shell, and lignite.

Jewelry

Jewelry and accessories were popular and consisted of fans, feather headdresses, beads in animal shapes, necklaces of tinkling bells, pendants, chest ornaments, leather and gold bands set with jade, and anklets. Poor people also wore the same kind of ornaments but substituted shells for precious stones. Feather cloaks were very highly valued and worn by the wealthy.

Boys had their ears and lips pierced during childhood and ear plugs and lip plugs of increasing size were inserted until a very heavy ear and lip ornament could be worn. Gold rods and precious stones were also worn in the nose.

Left: figure of woman wearing a wraparound skirt and ear spools.

21

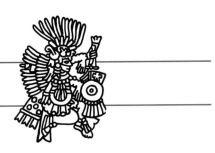

Religion and Rituals of the Aztecs

Aztec life was almost completely controlled by religion. Aztec religion involved group ceremonies designed to appease the gods. It had nothing to do with an individual's relationship with a god. The Aztecs also included the gods of other people in their own religion. Conquered people were given permission to retain their local gods provided Huitzilopochtli, the main Aztec god, was worshiped also.

Opposite: the figure of Quetzalcoatl, rising from the jaws of the feathered serpent. This figure is made of jade.

Below: handle of a sacrificial knife, made from wood and encrusted with turquoise and colored shell. The figure represents a kneeling deity.

Great ceremonies were performed at temples by priests on behalf of the people who assembled to watch. Since each Aztec god had a special ceremony, many were held. Ceremonies included dances, songs, processions, offerings, and dramas performed by masked priest actors.

Main Aztec Gods	
Huitzilopochtli	War and sun god.
Tezcatlipoca	Chief god of the Texcoco.
Quetzalcoatl	Feathered serpent, god of learning and priesthood.

Some Other Aztec Gods and Goddesses	
Tonatiuh	Sun god; his name is a title meaning "Royal Lord."
Coatlicue	Earth mother.
Teteoinnan	Mother of the gods.
Chicomecoatl	Goddess of vegetation.
Cihuacoatl	Earth goddess, goddess of fertility.
Centeotl	Maize god.
Xipe	"Our Lord the Flayed One," god of seed time and planting, god of sunset and sacrificial pain, god of suffering.
Xilonen	Princess of the unripe maize.
Tlaloc	Rain god (very important), god of all sources of water.
Chalchihuitlicue	Water goddess (very important).
Ehecatl	Lord of the winds.
Xuihtecuhtli	Lord of fire.
Mayahuel	Goddess of the maguey and also of fertility.
Patecatl	God of medicine.
Mictlantecuhtli	Lord of the dead.
Teoyaomiqui	God of dead warriors.
Xolotl	Monster god, twin of Quetzalcoatl.
Cihuateteô	Goddess of witches.

Mictlantecihuatl, consort of Mictlantecuhtli, Lord of the Underworld.

There were many other minor gods, and local gods and goddesses.

The Aztecs believed that mankind was created at the time of the fifth sun by Quetzalcoatl and his twin, Xolotl. This fifth world, the Aztecs thought, would be destroyed by an earthquake. They also believed that things were created from the bones of the dead as the sun and moon were created from the bodies of former gods, Nanahuatzin and Tecciztécal, who threw themselves into a fire.

The Beginning and Ending of the World

The Aztecs believed that the earth had been destroyed four times previously: the first time by jaguars, the second time by a hurricane which turned mankind into monkeys, the third time by rain, and the fourth time by flood. They believed that each destruction was caused by the death of the sun and, to prevent this from happening again, the sun had to be provided with human hearts and blood.

Temples, Priests, and Sacrifices

Each temple had a god. The hierarchy and duties of the priests are as follows:

Temple Hierarchy

High Priests	Administered all priests and temples. At the Great Temple were two high priests, the "priest of Tlaloc" and the "priest of Huitzilopochtli," each in the service of the two main gods.
Temple Priests	These priests in each temple offered guidance and prescribed ceremonies. Priests were assigned to special duties, such as being in charge of ceremonies, trainee priests, **astrology, divination,** temple lands, and education. Several grades of priesthood existed. Women could serve in the temple but were not allowed to perform sacrifices. Priests also performed self-sacrifice, which included bloodletting from their own ears and tongue.
Diviners	These people claimed to have supernatural powers. They often claimed to be able to transform themselves into other life forms. They used "magic" and "cast spells."

Sacrifices

Because the Aztecs believed that the sun needed blood to keep moving across the sky, and because they believed that new life was created from the bones of the dead, the Aztecs saw the need for human sacrifice. Prisoners of war were used in these ceremonies, and slaves were also bought for the purpose of sacrifice. Sometimes the Aztecs chose their own people to use as sacrificial victims. The Aztecs believed that the person sacrificed automatically gained eternal life. Victims were sacrificed with great ceremony, which usually involved cutting out their hearts. Victims were drowned or burned. Part of the victims' flesh was eaten as part of the ceremony. On some occasions thousands of victims were sacrificed.

The only Aztec temple to survive the Spanish conquest is in Santa Cecilia near Mexico City (Tenochtitlán). The structure on top of the temple is the god-house, in front of which sacrifices were performed.

Page from the codex, Fejervary-Mayer, which shows the fire god at the center of the universe, and the four world directions. The fire god is being fed on blood from sacrifices.

Death and Burial

The Aztecs believed the earth was the shape of a cross, and as such, the world had four directions. Each world direction had five of the twenty day signs, a color, and a god attached to it:

East—*acatl* (reed); red or green
West—*calli* (house); white
North—*tecpatl* (flint or knife); black
South—*tochtli* (rabbit); blue

A fifth point was the center of the cross and was attributed to the fire god.

Above the earth were thirteen heavens, of which the top was frozen. Here the supreme couple, the earth and the sun, lived. Under the earth were nine hells with nine rivers that the souls of the dead had to cross.

Upon death, the people who immediately went to heaven were the Quauhteca (Eagle People), those who were sacrificed or died in battle, those who died in faraway countries, and women who died having their first child. Warriors were believed to come back as hummingbirds after four years. All others went to hell, where they traveled for four years and finally disappeared.

Offerings were made to the dead eighty days after the funeral and, for the next four years, on the anniversary of the death, after which there was no further link with the dead.

Baptism

The Aztecs had a baptismal ceremony very similar to baptismal ceremonies held today. The head and lips of the baby were touched with water while the priest said, "That the sin, which was given to us before the beginnings of the world, might not visit the child, but that cleansed by these waters, it might live and be born again."

Christianity

Initially the Spanish were regarded as gods by the Aztecs, who had not seen Europeans or horses before. Aztec legends spoke of the return of Quetzalcoatl at the end of their fifty-two-year calendar cycle. The Spanish arrived at the end of this cycle. The Aztecs initially thought that a man riding on horseback was one creature, and that that creature was Quetzalcoatl.

After the Spanish conquest, the Catholic missionaries and friars attempted to convert all the Indians to Christianity. At first the Aztecs incorporated Christianity into their own religion, as they had always done. Although many Aztecs eventually became Christians, others retained their traditional religions and ceremonies.

Tlaloc, the rain god, to whom offerings were continually made so that he would send his messengers, the rain clouds, and bring fertility.

Obeying the Law

Aztec society was highly organized. Serving the gods, the emperor, and the clan was of utmost importance. As such there was very little personal freedom in Aztec society.

Tlatlacohtin

Craftsman

Merchant

Military commander

Snake woman

King

Structure of Aztec Society

Tlahtoani   The ruler had many titles, including "One who speaks." The ruler was elected from the same ruling family. No one was permitted to look directly at the ruler.

Three castes of Aztec society:

Pipiltin   Nobles by birth, members of the royal family, and professional warriors.

Macehualtin These were the common people who made up the majority of the population. Urban occupations were given a higher status than farming occupations. Commoners who captured four enemy warriors could be promoted to the rank of tecuhtli and assigned a private estate with serfs.

Mayehqueh Serfs who were attached to private or state rural estates.

Another element of society was:

Tlatlacohtin Poor men who could sell themselves or members of their family for a period of time. They had legal rights and were more like indentured servants or laborers than slaves.

Law and the Courts

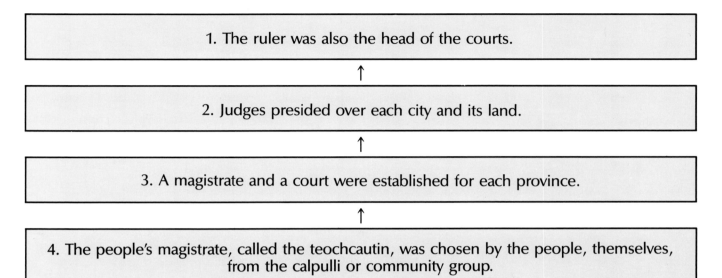

1. The ruler was also the head of the courts.

↑

2. Judges presided over each city and its land.

↑

3. A magistrate and a court were established for each province.

↑

4. The people's magistrate, called the teochcautin, was chosen by the people, themselves, from the calpulli or community group.

Right: an official passing judgment on a prisoner.

People reported any disorder or unfairness to the authorities. In some cities courts were held regularly, and in other places, only when necessary.

Some Crimes and Punishments

Judges could be put to death for taking a bribe. Murdering a slave was punishable by death. Theft was punishable by slavery or death. Drunkenness was punishable by death for young people. For older people property was confiscated. People could be enslaved for not paying their debts.

Other Aspects of the Law

Tlatlacohtin were given rights. They could have a family and own property and even own other slaves. Children of slaves were free and not thought of as being born into slavery.

Divorce was possible and both parties spoke before a court. The inability to bear children was considered grounds for divorce.

Families were responsible for teaching proper conduct to their children and punishments for children who disobeyed their parents were severe.

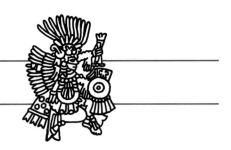

Writing It Down: Recording Things

The Aztecs kept records of trade and of the numbers and locations of the population. They also maintained maps of areas under Aztec control. Scribes were expected to keep registers of births and deaths, lists of rulers, religious rites and festivals, the calendar, and laws. These were written on a **codex,** which was strips of maguey paper or deer skin, folded like a screen. Maguey paper was made by soaking the fiber of the maguey cactus and beating and drying the pulp. Paper was also made from the bark of the amate or wild fig tree.

However, many Aztec records no longer exist, because they were destroyed by the Spanish.

Aztec Writing

The Aztecs did not have an alphabet but used hieroglyphic writing. Some of the glyphs or characters used were like miniature pictures of the object (see below). A great deal of information could be recorded this way.

Colors were used for adding more information, such as rushes being "written" in green, cane in blue, and grass in yellow, although the glyph or symbol might look the same.

Numbers

The Aztecs had a vigesimal system, that is, they counted by 20s.
1 to 19 were written as dots.
20 was written as a flag.
20 × 20 was written as a feather or fir tree.
20 × 20 × 20 was written as a bag or pouch.

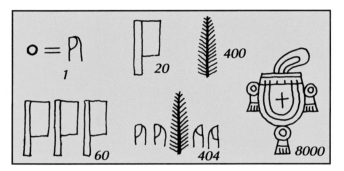

Measures

The Aztecs sold items by number or volume and not by weight.

troje = a bin holding about 200 tons (204 tonnes)

tlacopintli = a bin holding about 125–140 lbs. (56–63 kilograms).

Length

The basic unit was the span of a man's hand. Another measurement was a man's armspan and yet another, a measurement of height, was from the ground to as high as a person could reach above his head.

Value

Trade was done by **barter,** but sometimes people would accept cocoa beans as payment for small items. Payment was also made in goose quills full of gold dust or mantles of cloth.

The Calendar

The Aztec calendar was similar to that used by the Maya. It consisted of a ritual day cycle called *Tonalpohualli* and was based on a cycle of numbers from one to thirteen and a cycle of twenty day names. It could also be divided into four or five equal parts and assigned to a world quarter and a color. A list of twenty deities was associated with each cycle of thirteen days called the Lords of the Day and another thirteen deities called the Lords of the Night. Each had its own name and glyph. Special priests called Tonalpouhque were trained to interpret the calendar.

Aztec Day Signs

Cipactli (alligator)	Ozomatli (monkey)
Ehecatl (wind)	Malinalli (grass)
Calli (house)	Acatl (reed)
Cuetzpallin (lizard)	Ocelotl (ocelot)
Coatl (serpent)	Cuauhtli (eagle)
Miquiztli (death's head)	Cozcaquauhtli (vulture)
Mazatl (deer)	Ollin (motion)
Tochtli (rabbit)	Tecpatl (flint knife)
Atl (water)	Quiauitl (rain)
Itzcuintli (dog)	Xochitl (flower)

The Aztec solar year was adopted from the Maya. It had 365 days divided into eighteen named months, each month being made of twenty days. The additional five days (called nemontemi) that belonged to no month were considered unlucky. A year was named after the sacred day on which it began, such as "Feast of the Mountains" or "Fall of the Waters." The calendar was used to decide the time of festivals which occurred each month. The new year was celebrated by the making of a new fire. Every eight years the transit of Venus was celebrated.

Two 52-year cycles = "One Old Age" when the day cycle, the solar year, and the transit of Venus happened all together.

The famous "Calendar Stone" at the National Museum of Anthropology in Mexico shows the date when it was believed the earth would be destroyed again.

The Aztec Calendar: the wheel on the left has thirteen numbers. The wheel on the right has twenty named days. The wheel turns so that each day name fits with a number. The year begins with 1 rabbit. The next day is 2 water, and the following day is 3 dog, and so on until it gets to 13 flower. The left wheel is back to 1 and the cycle starts again with 1 alligator.

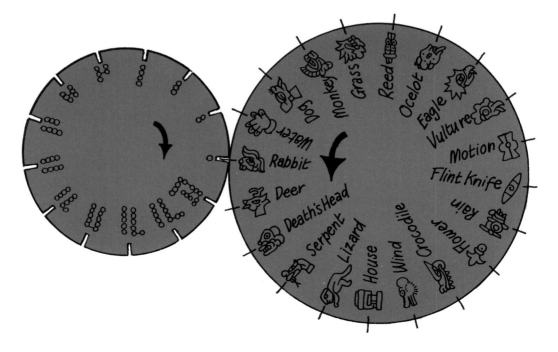

Aztec Legends and Literature

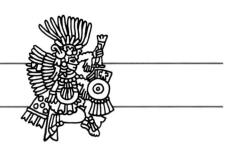

The Aztec system of writing was very basic and not flexible enough to record legends, poetry, and other literature, as abstract ideas could not be expressed. Not all children were taught to read and write, so learning from others and committing things to memory were very important. The Nahuatl literature, songs, speeches, stories of the gods, and the creation of earth were preserved in this way. In the sixteenth century A.D., when the Spanish taught people how to write using the alphabet, many of the hymns, verses, and songs were written down and preserved. Many, however, were lost as they were not written down and the Christian Spanish forbade many of the Aztec religious and social customs and the telling of stories that accompanied these.

The codices are one form of Aztec records that let us know about their rituals and legends. On the right, offerings are being made by the sun god, and by the god of darkness below. On the left, the planet Venus is shown attacking various social orders with darts.

Some Examples of Aztec Poetry

"My flowers shall not cease to live;
my songs shall never end:
I, the singer, intone them;
they become scattered, they are spread about."

Nezahualcoyotl.

"On seven ears, arise, awake. Our mother, thou leavest us now;
thou goest to thy home in Tlalocan.
Arise, awake. Our mother, thou leavest us now;
thou goest to thy home in Tlalocan."

Sahagun (in a song to the Maize Goddess)

"Where the burning, divine liquor is poured out,
where the divine eagles are blackened with smoke,
where the tigers roar,
where gems and rich jewels are scattered,
where precious feathers wave like spume,
there, where the warriors tear each other
and noble princes are smashed to pieces."

War poem describing a battlefield.

Art and Architecture

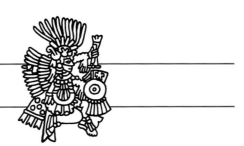

The Capital

The city of Tenochtitlán—Tlatelolco was built on islands in Lake Texcoco on land reclaimed from the swamps. The city had a population of about 350,000 people in A.D. 1519, which was larger than any European city at that time. It was linked by three causeways to the higher land, and two aqueducts brought fresh water into the city. A huge dike 10 miles (16 kilometers) long, with sluicegates, was built so the level of the lake could be controlled in times of floods. The city was divided into four sections:

Cuepopan—place where the flowers bloom;

Moyotla—place of the mosquitoes;

Atzacoalco—place of herons; and

Teopan—place of the gods.

The rectangular Temple Precinct in Teopan was enclosed by a wall decorated with serpent heads. Within the Temple Precinct was the skull rack, a special area containing the skulls of sacrificed victims. There was also a ball court, priests' rooms, rooms for fasting and punishments, and training rooms.

Here, too, was the Great Temple with its two shrines of Tlaloc and Huitzilopochtli in a pyramid 87 by 109 yards (80 by 100 meters) wide and rising to almost 30 yards (28 meters). Staircases wound up the sides of this pyramid. At the top of the pyramid stood the temples of the two gods. There were rooms, braziers, altars, and decorations for ceremonies of human sacrifices.

Here, also, were the grand palaces built by the Aztec rulers, such as the palace of Axayacatl, the "New Palace" built by Montezuma, and the Palace of Nezahualcoytl. These palaces were almost like small townships with some sitting rooms being capable of holding 3,000 people.

All the buildings stood amid gardens with canals, lakes, and bathing pools surrounding them.

Model of the city, Tenochtitlán. The layout of the city on the island in the lake is shown above the model.

Goldwork

Only a few gold objects have survived, such as gold disks, nose ornaments, and lip plugs. The German artist Albrecht Dürer saw some of the treasures of Montezuma (the Aztec king at the time of the Spanish conquest), which were taken by the Spanish. He praised the beauty and workmanship of these treasures. However, most of these treasures were melted down into ingots, and then shipped to Spain.

Featherwork

Feathers, especially those from rare birds, were highly prized by the Aztecs. They were used to decorate costumes, dresses for festivals and ceremonies, ornaments, headdresses for the leaders, and other smaller items such as fans.

Mosaics

Mosaics of stone and shell were used to decorate knives, masks, and shields, and frequently mosaics on a large scale were included in architectural decoration.

Ruins showing the image of the feathered serpent, which was central to the Aztec culture.

Lapidary Work

Most gems were obtained by trade. Jade, turquoise, and rock crystal were cut with copper tools using water and sand to help the cutting and polishing. Stones were usually set into jewelry or masks for religious festivals. Occasionally they were set into objects used in worship at the temple, and in shields and panels used for decorating buildings.

Sculpture

All the temples and courtyards were filled with sculpture and wall paintings. Most of the wall paintings were destroyed after the Spanish conquest, but some survived, including a mural in a temple at Malinalco and two altars from Tizatlan. Sculptures which have survived include the statue of the goddess, Coatlicue, the stone of Tizoc, and the Calendar Stone, which was the largest known Aztec carving. Other statues included those of the gods, important people, animals, birds, and various versions of Quetzalcoatl, models of the pyramids, and carved temple equipment.

Going Places: Transportation, Exploration, and Communication

The most common form of transportation for most Aztecs was walking. The Aztecs did not have wheeled vehicles. Loads were usually carried on people's backs.

An Aztec dugout canoe.

Boats

Canals took the place of roads in the Aztec capital and surrounding lands. Wooden dugout canoes were used on the lakes. So were flat-bottomed barges made of planks tied together. These were used for transporting produce and people along the canals and to local markets. Across land, the produce was carried on people's backs.

Trade

Professional merchants called **pochteca** undertook trade journeys of over a year in length and brought foreign goods back to the Aztec lands. These people also acted as spies in foreign places advising which towns could be attacked and conquered and the kinds of tribute to be gained from such a conquest.

A great trading guild eventually developed with its center at Tenochtitlán. Merchants also organized town markets.

Markets

These were important trade and commercial centers and people would walk long distances to reach them. Certain markets were well known for specializing in certain commodities. Acolman was famous for selling edible dogs, Azcapotzalco for birds and slaves, Cholula for fine work in feathers, and Texcoco for textiles and painted goods. The most famous market of all was in Tlaltelolco near the main temple.

Music, Dancing, and Recreation

Musical activities played a major part in Aztec life. Singing, dancing, and theater were popular entertainments. Musical instruments included clay whistles, pottery and bone flutes, drums, rattles, and bells. All boys and girls were taught singing, dancing, and music. A great variety of percussion instruments were played including:

The Huehuetl a large, vertical, skin-covered drum which could be tuned.

The Teponaztli a carved wooden gong or drum which had two tongues, each of which produced a different note when struck with a drum stick.

Other percussion instruments included drums made of tortoise or turtle shell and of carved wood, rattles of clay and wood, dried gourds containing seeds and pebbles, rattles made of wooden disks, and a rasp of bone which was scraped with a shell.

Copper bells and other objects were attached to dancers' clothing to make sounds as they moved.

The Aztecs did not have any stringed instruments.

Aztec music was not written down and not a single tune survives today.

Rich households had troupes of professional entertainers, dancers, clowns, jugglers, and stilt dancers. People also sang and played musical instruments for their own personal enjoyment. Feasts and festivals were times of music and dancing, and many religious dances were also dramas.

There were also dances not connected to religious celebration, such as handwaving, a dance performed in four rows without any musical accompaniment, and a "serpent dance" performed by young men and women.

The Spanish did everything possible to suppress the Aztec music and dancing fundamental to the Aztecs' religion, which the Christian Spanish wished to destroy.

Typical Aztec flageolets or small flutes.

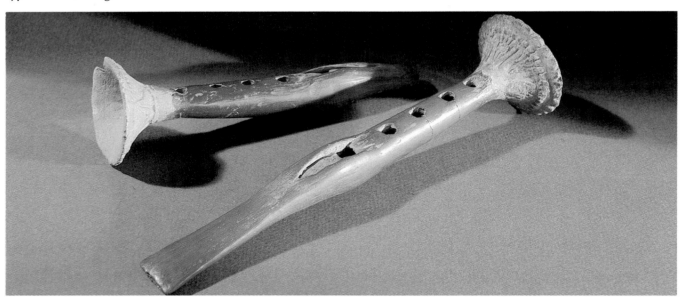

Aztec Festivals and Ceremonies

Name	Meaning	What Happened
Atlcoualo	Call for rain	Child sacrifice.
Tlacaxipeualiztli	Seedtime	Sacrifice of a prisoner.
Tozoztontli	Rain desired	Child sacrifices to Tlalocs and the earth mother to bring rain.
Hueitozoztli	Worship of new corn	Ceremonial bloodletting; young people dancing and singing.
Toxcatl	Rainy season begins	God impersonation ceremonies; captured warriors sacrificed.
Etzalqualiztli	Rain desired	Rain ceremonies, including the drowning of a boy and girl in a canoe filled with hearts of sacrificial victims.
Tecuilhuitontli	Rain desired	Salt workers were honored and salt was imported.
Hueitecuilhuitl	Great feast of rulers	Eight-day feast; women wore their hair loose; sacrifice of a slave, after which corn was eaten.
Tlaxochimaco	Birth of flowers	Feasts of turkey and corn cakes eaten to honor the god; dancing of men and women together.
Xocotlhuetzi	Fall of the fruits	Competitive climbing of a high pole by young men.
Ochpaniztli	Thanks to the earth mother	Sacrifice of woman impersonating the corn goddess; mock battles.
Teotleco	Return of the gods	Ceremonial honoring of the return of gods to the earth; ceremonial drinking and sacrifices.
Tepeilhuitl	Rain	Ceremonies for mountain rain gods; wooden snakes used in ceremony; sacrifice of four women.
Quecholli	Rain	Making of weapons; ceremonial hunt with sacrifice of game; feasting.
Panquetzaliztli	Winter solstice	Festivals honoring the war god; mock combats.
Atemoztli	Rain	Offerings to household gods; poles of streamers coated with rubber erected and burned to give off clouds of black smoke to tempt storm clouds to come.
Tititl	Season of stormy weather	Sacrifice of woman impersonating a goddess, weeping to bring rain; beating women with straw-filled bags to make them cry.
Izcalli	Toasting of the corn	Ceremonial hunt; killing of captives; killing of birds.

Weddings

These were festive occasions. Marriage was expected when a girl reached sixteen years of age and when a boy reached twenty years of age. The ceremony began in the evening by taking the bride to the groom's house. The bride was carried on the back of an old woman, while other women lighted the way with torches. The ceremony, itself, was held while the couple kneeled before the hearth with the bride's blouse knotted to the groom's cloak. After the ceremony came a celebration. The newly married couple were expected to pray and burn **incense** for four days after the ceremony.

Ball Games

These were played by the nobles, but common people came to watch. The game was played using a solid rubber ball in a long court enclosed by high walls. Goal rings were located on the side walls. Play was violent and players were frequently bruised and exhausted. Ritual ball games, which were thought to predict the outcome of events, were held also.

Board Games

A popular board game was patolli, a game similar to backgammon. People gambled on this game and invented all kinds of rituals, which were supposed to bring them luck.

The Volador or "Flying Place"

The **volador** was a spectacular entertainment consisting of a high pole and platform with four men dressed as birds attached by ropes to the corners of the frame at the top of the platform. At a given signal the men jumped from the platform, which rotated, making them "fly" around the pole thirteen times before touching the ground.

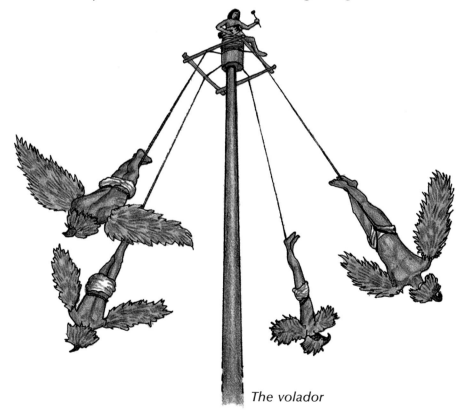

The volador

Wars and Battles

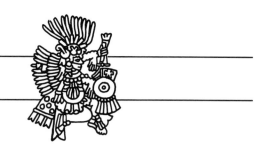

Warriors were highly regarded in Aztec society. The Aztecs were constantly engaged in battles, because they required a constant supply of raw materials, which could not be produced on their own lands. The Aztecs also needed a constant supply of victims for sacrifice at the temples. And unless the Aztecs maintained a strong army, they would have been attacked and conquered by others.

All men from age fifteen could be called upon to serve in the army. Warriors were not paid but were rewarded for special service by being given land, clothing, and slaves. Rulers usually led their armies to war. Each city or tribe raised an army of its own.

Summoning to Battle

Days and times of war were decided by the calendar priests. The priests, dressed in ceremonial dress and brandishing a shield, would then dance through the streets. At the same time the great war drum would sound. Warriors would immediately collect their weapons and assemble in front of the temple.

Scouts would be sent out in advance of the army to make sure that the warriors would not be ambushed. Priests carrying images of the gods would walk behind the leader into battle. Groups of warriors marched to war a day's march apart.

Warriors were accompanied by others as they marched to war: engineers who constructed ladders and bridges, people who prepared the food, and porters who carried stores and extra weapons. Food and supplies were offered by the people of the lands and villages through which the warriors passed.

Rules of Warfare

The object of a battle was not to kill the enemy but to take captives to sacrifice in the temple. Crops were not to be destroyed because control of the lands was needed. The people would then pay tribute in the form of precious stones, metals, and food.

Battles were short and fought in hand-to-hand combat like two teams. Chiefs directed the battle signaling with drums, whistles, pipes, and visible signals. When one side had obviously won, the warring ceased. Captives were counted and peace terms settled by the leaders. The Aztec army would return to victory celebrations.

War with the Spanish

The Spanish arrived in Aztec lands in 1519, and by 1521, the Aztec capital was in their control. The Spanish had superior weapons and horses and did not do battle according to the rules understood by the Aztecs. Although the Aztecs resisted and even won some battles, the Spanish were finally the victors.

Arms, Armor, and Ceremonial Dress

There was no special uniform. Warriors wore special shoulder ornaments and haircuts to show rank and achievement. Warriors in battle wore an armor of padded cotton, which was cooler and lighter than other armor and effective against enemy arrows. Weapons included the **javelin,** arrows, and **slings.** For close combat, a huge sword with a long blade made from obsidian was used. Spears were also used and occasionally hatchets and clubs.

The reception of Hernan Cortes by the emperor, Montezuma.

Each town had its tlacochcalco or "house of darts" near the main temple where weapons were stored.

A young man's head was clean-shaven except for a tuft of hair at the back, which could not be removed until the young warrior had taken a captive in battle. After a warrior had taken four captives, he was permitted the special hairstyle of the seasoned warrior. A different hairstyle and a patterned cloak showed that a warrior had captured a prisoner single-handedly. Shoulder ornaments also indicated how many captives a warrior had taken.

Captains carried standards of eagle feathers, fur, and red cord. Body ornaments indicated battles fought and captives taken, and jaguar skins indicated high rank.

Aztec Inventions and Special Skills

Chinampa Farming

The chinampas or "floating islands" were inventions of the Aztecs. Using this unique system of farming, the Aztecs made the muddy lakes and marshes of Lake Texcoco fertile and productive, and eventually the place of the capital city. This type of farming is still practiced today in some districts of Mexico City.

Featherwork

The famous Aztec featherwork was worked into spectacular mosaics. Feathers were from various tropical birds, such as parrots, hummingbirds, and the quetzal. The feathers were pasted on fine cotton and made into dresses, wall hangings, ornaments, headdresses, and cloaks.

Sacrifices

In the Aztec religion human and animal sacrifice had a central place. The people believed that the sun god needed a constant supply of human hearts and many different sacrificial ceremonies were performed. Sacrifice was thought of as giving the gods the most precious of all gifts, human life, and was considered a noble thing to do. The Aztecs attributed their prosperity to pleasing the gods and, as a result, sacrifices increased.

Using the Maguey Plant

This plant grew abundantly and the Aztecs put it to good use. The leaves were bruised, soaked, beaten, and dried to form a paper. A linenlike thread was also manufactured from the maguey and used for making clothes. An intoxicating drink called pulque was made from the juices of this plant. Thatch for the roofs of houses was also made from maguey. The tough plant fibers were used to make strong cords and the thorns were turned into pins and needles. Even the roots were cooked and eaten.

Cochineal Beetle

The Aztecs learned to use the cochineal beetle which lived on the cactus plantations. It was often specially kept and raised. A bright crimson color was extracted from the beetle and used to dye fabrics. This knowledge was later taken to Europe.

A Unifying Religion

The worship of the sun god was common to all people who lived in Aztec lands. Their beliefs and practices made the world seem logical and meaningful, and as everyone was anxious to please the sun god, they all had some common behavior.

Why the Civilization Declined

Although the Aztecs were a warlike people who were used to invasions and invading, the conquering of their lands by the Spanish changed their civilization completely.

Most of the Spanish who came to Aztec lands with Cortes were greedy for wealth and power and exploited the land and the people in an uncaring way. Many Aztecs were killed in battle while serving the Spanish.

Others, such as the Christian missionaries, were determined to stamp out the Aztecs' pagan religion and replace it with Christianity, and as a result, took away from the people something that made life meaningful. The Aztecs felt bewildered by the loss because religion and its rituals had played a central part in their lives. Furthermore, they were often punished for not observing the Christian religion in a way acceptable to the Spanish.

The Spanish also replaced the old ways of learning with a Spanish Christian education, and eventually the old ways of thinking and behaving were replaced and almost forgotten.

Diseases to which the Aztecs had no resistance were passed on from the Spanish to the native people. Many thousands died as a result of the devastating epidemics of smallpox, measles, and influenza. In some places 80 percent of the population died.

The Spanish men often married Indian women, and the population gradually changed as it incorporated those of mixed blood.

However, the Aztecs did manage to retain some of their ancient ways, including the worship of their pagan gods, their farming methods, and market days. Other social customs and traditional dress are still honored by descendants of the Aztecs today. Although this unique civilization that had developed in the Mexico Valley was changed by the Spanish invasion, aspects of it have survived.

Spanish cathedral in Mexico—the Spanish imposed their religion, Christianity, on the Aztecs and were responsible for destroying the Aztec religion and way of life.

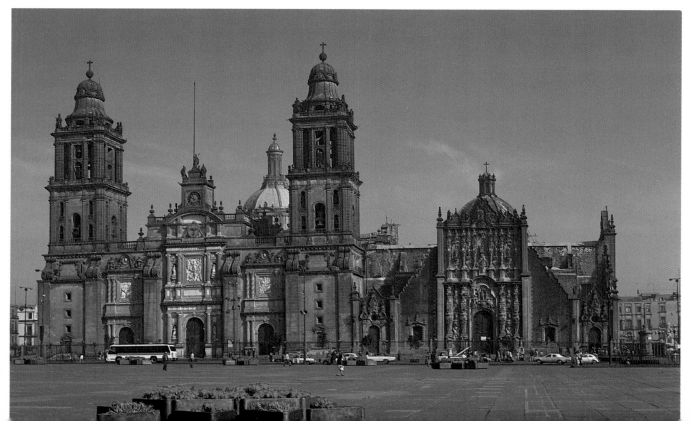

Glossary

Adobe A brick made of silt or clay deposited by rivers and then dried in the sun.

Astrology A study which holds the belief that the position of the stars and other heavenly bodies has an influence on human affairs.

Barter To trade by exchange of goods instead of using money. The Aztecs did not have money.

Cálmecac Higher school.

Calpulli Community groups into which families were organized. Each calpulli was ruled by the heads of all households making up the calpulli.

Chinampa farming A chinampa is an artificial island made by scooping up mud and vegetation and holding it in an area by stakes, reeds, and trees. Canals are formed between these islands. Crops are grown on these islands. In this way land is reclaimed from marshes and made productive.

Coa A digging stick.

Codex A manuscript or book. It was made of paper from the maguey plant or the bark of the wild fig tree. It consisted of a long narrow strip about 4 inches high and many yards long and folded like a fan or concertina. Plural *codices*.

Coyote A wild, wolflike animal.

Divination An attempt to discover the future or to decide the outcome of events by supernatural means or a prophecy based on chance. Methods used included counting grains, observing the movements of insects or birds in flight, or smoke. Divination does not use logical reasoning.

Dry farming A type of farming practiced in areas of low rainfall. It uses methods of soil tilling that reduce the amount of evaporation from the soil but allow the plants to obtain oxygen, which is needed for growth.

Gourd A fruit or vegetable grown by the Aztecs. The shell was often dried and used as a container or as a percussion instrument.

Granadilla A fruit similar to a passion fruit.

Hearth That part of the floor on which or above which the cooking fire is placed.

Incense A substance that produces a perfume or strong spicy smell when burned. It is usually burned during religious ceremonies.

Javelin An Aztec throwing spear used in battle. It was thrown by means of an atl-atl, or throwing board, which enabled it to be thrown farther and with greater force.

Maguey (Also called agave). A cactus which grew wild and was cultivated by the Aztecs and used for food, clothing, paper, and as building material.

Mosaic A picture or decoration made of small pieces of stone, shell, and precious stones of different colors fixed to a surface.

Obsidian A dark volcanic glass used for making tools, blades, and spear points.

Ocelot A South American animal. A spotted leopardlike cat.

Papaya A pawpaw.

Pimento A tropical American tree. The fruit, also called pimento, is used as a spice.

Pochteca The Aztec name given to the professional merchants.

Quetzal A colorful bird with long tail feathers which were highly prized by the Aztecs.

Sling A weapon of war used to hurl stones and other missiles with great force. It consisted of a piece for holding the missile, and two strings. The strings were held in the hand. The sling was whirled rapidly and the stone or missile released.

Sluicegates A gate at the end of an artificial channel or canal which can be opened or shut to control the amount of water flowing through.

Tamale A dish made of crushed maize (and perhaps meat) seasoned with peppers or chilies, wrapped in maize husks and cooked.

Telpochcalli A school for young men from age fifteen onwards where they were instructed in the duties of manhood and use of weapons of war.

Tititl Healer.

Tortilla A thin, round, flat cake made from maize flour and baked on flat stones or another surface. It was eaten with beans and chilies.

Trident An instrument or weapon with three prongs at the end. It was used by the Aztecs to spear fish.

Volador The "flying place."

The Aztecs: Some Famous People and Places

MONTEZUMA II

Montezuma, born A.D. 1466 and died 1520, was the last Aztec emperor of Mexico and famous for his stand against the Spanish conquistador, Hernan Cortes. Montezuma succeeded his uncle, Ahuitzotl, as leader of the Aztec empire in 1502. The empire reached its peak at this time, but was becoming weaker because of increased demands on the conquered people to provide more tribute and more victims for sacrifices.

The Aztecs, especially Montezuma, feared the return of their white-bearded god, Quetzalcoatl. The Aztecs mistook Cortes for Quetzalcoatl because Cortes arrived in the last year of the Aztecs' fifty-two-year calendar. This was the year that the Aztecs feared Quetzalcoatl would return. Cortes used this fear to his advantage and eventually made Montezuma his prisoner.

TENOCHTITLÁN

This was the Aztec capital built on an island on Lake Texcoco. Originally the island comprised two cities, Tlatelolco and Tenochtitlán, but these merged into one. About 350,000 people were living in the capital in 1519, when Cortes arrived. He conquered the city, razed it, and constructed a Spanish city on its ruins. The new city, Mexico City, was officially recognized in 1522.

CORTES

Hernan Cortes was the Spanish conqueror of Mexico. He arrived in Mexico in 1519. After his arrival Cortes burned his ships, which committed his forces to the conquest of the land.

Cortes captured a princess who spoke Nahuatl, the Aztec language, and she became his interpreter and adviser. She was called Dona Marina by the Spanish. Without her help Cortes probably would not have succeeded.

Montezuma had welcomed Cortes to the capital, Tenochtitlán. When Cortes realized he and his men had been trapped in the city, he made Montezuma his prisoner, knowing that while he did this, the Aztecs would not attack his men. The Aztecs, however, regarded Montezuma's capture as defeat and lost their respect for him. Montezuma died within three days, and the Aztecs believed he had been murdered by the Spanish. As Cortes and his men tried to escape from the capital, they were almost overcome and killed.

Later, Cortes eventually attacked and destroyed the capital. He conquered it street by street. By 1521 the Spanish had defeated the Aztec empire.

MONTE ALBAN

Monte Alban is a ruined city in present-day Oaxaca. It was built originally in about the eighth century and contains great plazas, pyramids, and a ball court, underground passages, and nearly 170 tombs. The great plaza is on top of the highest hill and is surrounded by four platforms with two temples standing to the south.

BERNARDINO DE SAHAGUN

Bernardino de Sahagun was a Spanish historian and missionary who spent most of his life in Mexico. His work, entitled *Historia General de las Cosas de Nueva España*, covered all aspects of Aztec culture, including religion, folk medicine, botany, and economics. The book was written in the Aztec pictorial language as well as in Spanish. It was written, on order, to assist Spanish missionaries with converting people to Christianity and to make their jobs more effective.

ANAHUAC

Anahuac is a district in the center of Aztec Mexico. Its name in Nahuatl means "Land by the Water." The area consisted of five interlocking lakes when the Spanish arrived. The names of these lakes were Xaltocan, Texcoco, Xochimilco, Zumpango, and Chalco and in their midst stood the Aztec capital, Tenochtitlán. The water from the lakes has been drained over the centuries.

LAKE TEXCOCO

This is the largest and lowest lake in central Mexico and was originally one of five lakes. It was originally called by its mystical name, Metzliapan, or "Moon Lake." The Aztecs managed to convert a portion of this lake to fresh water. The Aztec capital, Tenochtitlán, stood on islands in Texcoco, connected to the mainland by causeways. Since the seventeenth century, Lake Texcoco has been drained, and it now only occupies a small area surrounded by salt marshes.

IXTLILXÓCHITL

Ixtlilxóchitl was an Aztec chieftain of the Texcoco who supported the Spanish conquistador Cortes in the overthrow of the Aztecs in Tenochtitlán. Through his efforts the capital eventually fell to the Spanish, Ixtlilxóchitl remained an ally of the Spanish, but he eventually lost the respect of his people. He was also an historian, writer, and translator and many of his works survived until after the Spanish conquest.

AZCAPOTZALCO

Azcapotzalco was a state on the lake shore to which the Aztecs originally paid tribute and continued to do so until the end of the reign of Chimalpopoca, who was assassinated by Maxtla, ruler of Azcapotzalco. However, the power of this state was soon broken.

The area later became famous for its slave market and the skill of its craftsmen who worked in precious metals. It was here Cortes later set up smelters to melt treasure into bullion before shipping it back to Spain. The Spanish also destroyed the Aztec temple and on the site built a convent.

POPOCATÉPETL

This is a volcano 18,045 feet (5,500 meters) high in the Aztec homelands which has a permanent snowcap. Its name means "Smoking Mountain." Cortes and his men are thought to have been the first to climb its peak in 1519.

Index

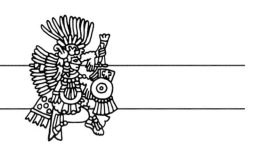